A Splash of Water

A Splash of Water

The Haiku Society of America
Members' Anthology 2015

Catherine J.S. Lee, Editor

Published by
The Haiku Society of America
New York, New York
October 2015

A Splash of Water

ISBN: 978-1-930172-13-5

Each poem in this anthology was chosen by the editor from
a selection of unpublished and published haiku submitted by
current members of The Haiku Society of America. Each
participating member has one poem in the anthology.

Designed and produced by Catherine J.S. Lee
in collaboration with Mike Montreuil. Thank you to
David Lanoue and the HSA for inviting me to edit this
anthology. It was a pleasure and a privilege.

Titles: Kaushan Script
Text: Cochin

Cover and interior photographs by Catherine J.S. Lee

Introduction

Here in Maine, where it's frequently said, "If you don't like the weather, wait a minute," 2015 brought a summer of little rain. On the opposite coast of North America, California experienced its fourth summer of drought and in the midwest, the depletion of the mighty Ogallala Aquifer continues. Water scarcity is an increasing worldwide concern, impacting over two billion people for at least one month of the year.

Water is life, and the number of haiku that have been written about it in its myriad forms attests to the fact that it's an important subject for poets as well as farmers and fishermen. Water in all its forms—salty ocean and sweat and tears, freshwater lakes and rivers and ponds and pools and fountains, rain and snow and fog and ice—is a major source of inspiration. For me, reading the nearly three hundred submissions to this year's anthology was a never-ending experience of surprise and delight at how this important element affects us all, sustaining and refreshing not only the body but also the soul.

I could write here about my selection and arrangement processes, but you, dear reader, would make better use of your time by reading the haiku themselves. My fellow Mainer, Stephen King, once wrote, "It is the tale, not he who tells it." I would amend that to say, "It is the haiku, not she who chose them." I hope you enjoy the book I put together for you.

Catherine J.S. Lee
Eastport, Maine, USA
October, 2015

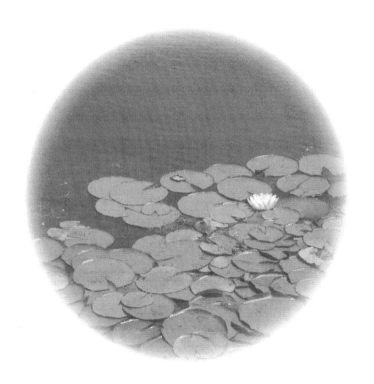

Freshwater

rising river
a shadow still wedged
between the rocks

~ *Susan Constable, Nanoose Bay, British Columbia, Canada*

mountain pool
the trout points the way
to the glacier

~ *Marsh Muirhead, Bemidji, Minnesota*

a lily pad
pulled back to its stem
cold spring wind . . .

~ *Bruce Ross, Hampden, Maine*

the rain ends . . .
from the darkening swamp
a hermit thrush

~ Cor van den Heuvel, New York, New York

her first pregnancy
water falls down the mountain
into swelling creeks

~ Jeanne Jorgensen, Edmonton, Alberta, Canada

rain lifts my little boat
I trail my oars and let
the waters let me go

~ Robert Witmer, Tokyo, Japan

melting ice
rushes over the stones-
Inuit throat song

~ Sue Colpitts, Peterborough, Ontario, Canada

spring fever
skunk cabbage burns a hole
in the ice pocket

~ Nola Obee, Armstrong, British Columbia, Canada

spring breeze
my fishing rod catches
the moon

~ John J. Han, Manchester, Missouri

White clouds
floating on water mirror
shattered by boot

~ *John-Carl Davis, West Bend Wisconsin*

her toe-tip in the lake
the slender bough
of a budding tree

~ *Wanda D. Cook, Hadley, Massachusetts*

a gust
minnow kites twirl
onto the pond

~ *Jeffrey McMullen, Cuba, New York*

icemelt
the gorge releases
frozen sound

~ *Mark Dailey, Poultney, Vermont*

first stars—
along the river road
choirs of peepers

~ *Kathe L. Palka, Flemington, New Jersey*

snowmelt
the cascading notes
of a canyon wren

~ *Tom Painting, Atlanta, Georgia*

stepping
in the same stream twice
just as cold

~ *David Gershator, St. Thomas, Virgin Islands*

spring gusts
a million suns
on the rippling pond

~ *Jim Laurila, Florence, Massachusetts*

cherry blossoms
drift into the lake
the white swan

~ *Nancy Brady Huron, Ohio*

13

one breath near
the sound of water on rock
scent of lilacs

~ *Adam T. Arn, Belgium, Wisconsin*

our walk home
sound of the creek
through gaps in the ice

~ *Robert Forsythe, Annandale, Virginia*

river in flood
a heron lifts
from the bruised bank

~ *Lynne Rees, Offham, Kent, UK*

black phoebe
visits the empty pool
spring rain

~ Janis Albright Lukstein, Palos Verdes Peninsula, California

three springs later
the abandoned house
still bears the flood's scars

~ Dorothy McLaughlin Somerset, New Jersey

after spring rain ends:
path to the creek
sandbagged after I last walked past

~ Patti Niehoff, Cincinnati, Ohio

spring rain
the brook bubbles faster
to the waterfall

~ *susan major-tingey, Quincy, Massachusetts*

spring brook awakens
whispering all
its winter dreams

~ *Irene K. Wilson, Lexington, Massachusetts*

four short blasts
Bakken oil train warns
the bay's otters

~ *Rich Schnell, Port Douglas, New York*

water sounds . . .
my memory wanders the coast
of a summer lake

~ *Carmen Sterba, University Place, Washington*

wading the shallows
blush on the belly
of a little blue heron

~ *Cherie Hunter Day, Cupertino California*

the dry riverbed –
I join a millennium
of conversation

~ *Phil Allen, Hartland, Wisconsin*

cutting open
the golden trout
lake's alpine glow

~ *Marcyn Del Clements, Claremont, California*

dawn swim--
making a butterfly of water
of light

~ *Kristen Deming, Bethesday, Maryland*

sunrise:
out of the river an osprey
clutches silver

~ *Ruth Yarrow, Ithaca, New York*

dragonfly on my fly rod both of us fishing

~ *Stuart Barlow, Salem, New York*

```
miles
 to
  the
  water
  fall
   a
    river
     runs
      down
       my
        spine
```

~ *Lorin Ford, Melbourne, Victoria, Australia*

night swimming a path to the moon

~ *Deb Koen, Rochester, New York*

my garden pond
plucked a full moon –
two floating lilies

~ *Neal Whitman, Pacific Grove, California*

old blue car
a shimmer of clouds
in the hose water

~ *Chad Lee Robinson, Pierre, South Dakota*

the bent pine
shades the trout pool...
no frog insight

~ *Randall Herman, Lyons, Nebraska*

August mountaintop
  cool water
    slides over my tongue

> ~ *Judith Hishikawa, West Burke, Vermont*

slow creek
flows into silence
fireflies

> ~ *James A. Paulson, Narberth, Pennsylvania*

clouds of insects
my thoughts narrow
into a river

> ~ *Glenn G. Coats, Prospect, Virginia*

long day
slap of the river
against a dock

~ *Michael Blottenberger, Hanover, Pennsylvania*

after the torrent
the all clear
cicadas

~ *Caroline Giles Banks, Minneapolis, Minnesota*

gently flowing water
the word she
utters . . .

~ *Hema, Chennai, Tamil Nadu, India*

kiddie pool
floating
into childhood memories

~ *Julie A. Riggott, Glendale, California*

old pond
choked with weeds
turtle nose on top

~ *Jim Applegate, Roswell, New Mexico*

lake house dusk
fireflies swimming
in the kids' eyes

~ *Lesley Clinton, Sugar Land, Texas*

through the cottonwoods
the river moves under gold
summer eve

~ *Shelley Baker-Gard, Portland, Oregon*

quiet lake
water snakes swim inside
the safety lines

~ *Eric Arthen, Worthington Massachusetts*

water scorpion
the pond exposed
by torchlight

~ *Tim Gardiner, Manningtree, Essex, UK*

dancing until dawn
by the lily-bordered lake
a murmur of air

~ Joanne M. Reinbold, Wilmington, Delaware

feeding frenzy
in swift strokes
koi paint the pond

~ Catherine Anne Nowaski, Rochester, New York

wild strawberries
we go skinny-dipping
at the end of the hike

~ RaNae Merrill, New York, New York

paddling home
blue moon drifting out
of a boathouse

~ Jennifer Thiermann, Glenview, Illinois

a dip in
the neighbor's pool
the moon and me

~ Juliet Seer Pazera New Orleans, Louisiana

misty daisies
engulf the mountain brook
dad's fishing coat

~ Dana Quick-Naig, Johnston, Iowa

lake swim
the hidden depths
of my dismay

~ Michele Root-Bernstein, East Lansing, Michigan

kayaking
the weight of the river
in her arms

~ Doris Lynch, Bloomington, Indiana

record heat
two kingfishers stake claim
to the salmon stream

~ Billie Wilson, Juneau, Alaska

willow tree
beside the lake
croaking frogs

~ *Dennise Aiello, Benton, Louisiana*

sky in the pond
a snakebird dries
its wings

~ *Brad Bennett, Arlington, Massachusetts*

reaching summer's end
a newspaper boat sets sail
for the horizon

~ *Poppy Herrin, Gonzales, Louisiana*

breathless afternoon
the water spider's ripples
going nowhere

~ Dina E. Cox, Unionville, Ontario, Canada

lapwings
rounding up clouds
left in the water

~ Alan Summers, Bradford on Avon, Wiltshire, England

imagining
you love me —
bubbling creek

~ Susan Burch, Hagerstown, Maryland

a stream so still
the only sound
lovers whispering in the night

~ *Audrey G. Olberg, Chevy Chase, Maryland*

riding the downwind
edge of a catamaran
life in the fast lane

~ *E. Luke, Palos Verdes Peninsula, California*

a night's reflections
into the river flow —
walking off the blues

~ *Ellen Compton, Washington, DC*

the small brook cascades
far into the mountain pool
        bubble flotilla

~ *Arch Haslett, Toronto, Ontario, Canada*

iron skillet at the ready trout fishing

~ *Patricia Wakimoto, Gardena, California*

in quiet water
at sunset   fish rise
the clouds quiver

~ *Ann M. Penton, Green Valley, Arizona*

autumn breeze—
the river winds
around the bend

~ Karen O'Leary, West Fargo, North Dakota

wood knot
in my pocket—
fog over water

~ Marilyn Fleming, Pewaukee, Wisconsin

roar of white water
beyond the canyon walls
the Milky Way

~ Barbara Snow, Eugene, Oregon

wake of a mallard
each exhalation
a little longer

~ *Sharon Pretti, San Francisco, California*

mother's ashes
the lake reflects
a shooting star

~ *Peg McAulay Byrd, Madison, New Jersey*

from poplar to pine
a cormorant
divides the river fog

~ *Janelle Barrera, Key West, Florida*

smooth glide
of wood ducks on the lake
your promises

~ Scott Wiggerman, Albuquerque, New Mexico

still we stand
first autumn wind
off the lake

~ Nicholas M. Sola, New Orleans, Louisiana

ancient starlight
in my newborn's eyes
leaves on a river

~ Steve Hodge, White Lake, Michigan

first nation
the passing on
of salmon to river

~ *Michelle Schaefer, Bothell, Washington*

autumn pool
water so clear I see
only bottom

~ *John Quinnett, Bryson City, North Carolina*

a heavy fog —
on every twig of every branch,
droplets of street light

~ *Dean Summers, Seattle, Washington*

branches sweeping
the darkness of water --
your breath on my skin

~ Michelle Tennison, Blackwood, New Jersey

causeway complete
a muskrat's wet tail
reconnects the river

~ LeRoy Gorman, Napanee, Ontario, Canada

this long grieving
water drops glisten
on the backs of ducks

~ Margaret Chula, Portland, Oregon

a blade of water...
carving canyons
from stone

~ *Jo Balistreri, Genesee Depot, Wisconsin*

river stones
cold in the hand
falling light

~ *Harry Goodheart, Tryon, North Carolina*

old brown bear
feeling the cloudpath
in the brook

~ *C.R. Harper, Seattle, Washington*

ice floes . . .
the wren's many poses
on the reed

~ *Allan Burns, Colorado Springs Colorado*

the indifference
of the brook
penetrating drizzle

~ *Klaus-Dieter Wirth, Viersen, NRW, Germany*

January lake
bobbing at dusk
duck laughter

~ *Peter Meister, Huntsville, Alabama*

muddy river
your voice
in the winter reeds

~ Renée Owen, Sebastopol, California

frigid lake
half-submerged log
where turtles once sunned

~ William F. Schnell, Aurora, Ohio

a squall approaches
slowly darkness
swallows the lake

~ William Hart, Montrose California

Almost within grasp
a sprinkle of stars
on the frozen river

~ *Sylvia Forges-Ryan, North Haven, Connecticut*

frozen pond the frog in my throat

~ *Johnny Baranski, Vancouver, Washington*

writer's block
my walk circles
the reservoir

~ *Christopher Patchel, Chicago, Illinois*

On the frozen pond
the wind's
signature

~ *Alexis Rotella, Arnold, Maryland*

mid way through winter
and no one in the canyon
water under ice

~ *Gary Schroeder, Franktown, Colorado*

captured by
frozen water
one branch

~ *Nancy Wells, Damascus, Pennsylvania*

winter sunshine
each creek stone's song
a sparkle

~ *Robert Gilliland, Austin, Texas*

river captures dusk
the exact blue of
manhattan bridge

~ Michelle Spadafore, Brooklyn New York

stitching the darkness
the glint
of a gondola's prow

~ Scott Mason, Chappaqua, New York

reflection pond
the color of the shadows
under the child's eyes

~ Dianne Garcia, Seattle Washington

hills rising
from opposite shores
the river's grace

~ *Mike Montreuil, Ottawa, Ontario, Canada*

red-eye gravy sunset over the bayou

~ *Alan S. Bridges, Littleton, Massachusetts*

the age of the river a ripple in stone

~ *Peter Newton, Winchendon, Massachusetts*

house on a canal
the smell of oil
on scattered boat parts

~ *John Russo, Key West, Florida*

Ocean

still no rain —
within the estuary's mist
the bark of a seal

~ *Lew Watts, Santa Fe, New Mexico*

afternoon slump
an overcast sky slips
into the sea

~ *Sondra J. Byrnes, Santa Fe, New Mexico*

drifting clouds . . .
the ocean bursts into
a gull's cry

~ *Sandip Chauhan, Great Falls, Virginia*

waves washing
the sandcastle away . . .
waning summer

~ Olivier Schopfer, Geneva, Switzerland

crabbing with my adult daughter
we throw the trap
into dark water

~ Mac Green, Indianapolis, Indiana

ocean's edge
the sandal's sole
worn thin

~ Scott Glander, Glenview, Illinois

windsurfing
the taste of ocean
in each breath

~ *Joe McKeon, Strongsville, Ohio*

orange juice
with a slice of lime
bird-crazy beach

~ *Michael Fessler, Sagamihara, Kanagawa, Japan*

swimmer that I was —
the phosphorescence
of southern seas

~ *Ruth Holzer, Herndon Virginia*

after the dredging
amidst gulls and coots,
the kingfisher's dive

~ *Richard Bruns, Napa, California*

at every angle of repose shorebirds

~ *Carolyn Hall, San Francisco, California*

ocean waves —
the constant pounding
of nails

~ *Rob Dingman, Herkimer, New York*

only our breathing
and the waves' whispers
summer's end

~ *Joan Prefontaine, Cottonwood, Arizona*

underwater slip
still a blue tip
to the oar

~ *Marshall Hryciuk, Toronto, Ontario, Canada*

hibiscus blossom
my body unfolds
into the pacific

~ *Brent Goodman, Rhinelander, Wisconsin*

a year later
sail boats still glide
across the cottage wall

~ *Marylouise Knight, Omaha, Nebraska*

nap on the beach—
the siren sound
of the waves

~ *Joette Giorgis, Port St. Lucie, Florida*

breaking wave—
a surfer tangles in
sunset's rose ribbons

~ *Tim Happel, Iowa City, Iowa*

boneyard
a ship's skeleton
sails in the sand

~ *Diane Wallihan, Port Townsend, Washington*

low tide . . .
I sift through the detritus
from another shore

~ *Carole MacRury, Point Roberts, Washington*

water aerobics class
the taste of the sea
off Greece

~ *Brenda Lempp, Madison, Wisconsin*

low tide –
a watermelon seed path
to the sandcastle

~ *Angelee Deodhar, Chandigarh, UT, India*

shushed by crashing waves
the shouts of children
hunting moonlit crabs

~ *Anna Eklund-Cheong, Croissy-sur-Seine, France*

the scent
of the sea at dusk . . .
Indian summer

~ *Damir Janjalija, Belgrade, Serbia*

daybreak
beneath a mackerel sky
the splash of oars

~ *Carolyn Coit Dancy, Pittsford, New York*

late September--
where the sea ends
a broken shell
(In Memory of Ken Leibman)

~ *Marian Olsonn, Santa Fe, New Mexico*

incoming waves
paint the rocky shoreline
full moon white

~ *Anthony T. Green, Lacey, Washington*

how silent
the pull of the moon
ebb tide

~ *Jeannie Martin, Arlington, Massachusetts*

between dark clouds
and a darker sea
rising mist

~ *Edith Bartholomeusz, Pearland, Texas*

all night tidal flows:
Orion reflected in
its serene surface

~ *Tom Hahney, Bellingham, Washington*

a baby turtle
returned to the sea
December moon

~ *Angela Terry, Lake Forest Park, Washington*

distant sea lions singing heavy snowfall

~ *Lyle Rumpel, Victoria, British Columbia, Canada*

frozen bay fishing
the eerie sound of
ice cracking

~ *Ronald Grognet, New Orleans, Louisiana*

the osprey's dive
spot-on
the life I had

~ *Seren Fargo, Bellingham, Washington*

rockbound bay —
a black swan emerges
from the sound of fog

~ *Lysa Collins, White Rock, British Columbia, Canada*

bitter cold —
on the beach, fossils frozen
in the sand

~ *Robert Ertman, Annapolis, Maryland*

winter sea
an osprey sails
into endless sky

~ *Catherine J.S. Lee, Eastport, Maine*

Rockaway Beach
mom's memory recedes
with the waves

~ *Robert Epstein, El Cerrito, California*

harbor lights—
black water shimmers
on a starless night

~ *Patricia Prine, Maywood Illinois*

alone
on the open sea…
the splash of a haiku

~ Mary Ellen Rooney, New York, New York

white caps fan out
in constant motion
ocean's pulse

~ Gloria Ayvazian, Northampton, Massachusetts

the morning after
the golden sunset photos—
a muddy tide flat

~ Rick Clark, Seattle, Washington

rough seas —
reading *Moby Dick*
in the bathtub

~ *David Lanoue, New Orleans, Louisiana*

receding tide in the rocks part of each wave

~ *Adelaide B. Shaw, Millbrook, New York*

a line of gulls
fencing the shoreline
unbroken sun

~ *David Jacobs, London, England*

waves
washing over rocks—
moonlight remains

~ *John Gonzalez, Ipswich, Suffolk, England*

north coast—
listening to the wind and waves
to hear each other

~ *Bruce H. Feingold, Berkeley, California*

ebbing tide
I let go of dreams
that no longer fit

~ *Patricia Pella, Woodland, California*

Along the waterfront
women in windows
stained by the sea

~ *Dave Sutter, San Francisco, California*

lost in the tide
my pen drifts away
with my thoughts

~ *Carole Slesnick, Bellingham Washington*

lines of foam —
over and over the sea
writes its story

~ *Annette Makino, Arcata, California*

above the bay
swallows skim the surface--
first draft

~ S.M. Kozubek, Chicago, Illinois

quiet beach
I release my breath to the tide

~ Bill Sette, Arlington, Virginia

ashes afloat—
memories of reefs
we snorkeled

~ Dan Daly, Ballwin, Missouri

enough said . . .
the moon rises
out of the sea

~ *Francine Banwarth, Dubuque, Iowa*

every time
i think of you
the pull of tides

~ *Michael Rehling, Presque Isle, Michigan*

wind — countless seagulls
drift randomly above
silver waves

~ *Neil Schaefer, Scotts Valley, California*

we promise each other
nothing will change
slack tide

~ *Deborah P Kolodji, Temple City, California*

the tide turns—
a hem of spume lace
brushes my feet

~ *Suzanne Niedzielska, Glastonbury, Connecticut*

rendezvous . . .
two moons following
in footprint tide pools

~ *Robert Sorrels, Brazil, Indiana*

tide rip —
the slant of light
through the islands

~ Michael Dylan Welch, Sammamish, Washington

wrecked boat
resting between boulders
gently lapping sea

~ Robert Muroff, Long Beach Township, New Jersey

shells in a glass lamp
international oceans
crashing beside me

~ Nancy Shires, Greenville North Carolina

Weather

homecoming
old wheelbarrow full
of spring rain

~ *Matthew Caretti, Mercersburg, Pennsylvania*

breath of sunrise
aroma of spring rain yet to fall

~ *Barbara Tate, Winchester, Tennessee*

Spring rain
blue irises cover her
patchwork skirting

~ *Heather Munn, Reynoldsburg, Ohio*

spring flurries
a half-built wren's nest
filling with snow

~ Elizabeth Howard, Crossville, Tennessee

shaking themselves
newly shorn sheep
stare at puddles

~ Kevin Goldstein-Jackson, Poole, Dorset, England

cascading rains
the arms of the old willow
pointing the way home

~ Patricia Noeth, Iowa City, Iowa

awake
at three a.m. on purpose
—spring rain

~ *Alison Woolpert, Santa Cruz, California*

day long spring rain
even the artificial turf
seems greener

~ *William Seltzer, Gwynedd, Pennsylvania*

April showers
our rain boots
covered in snow

~ *Amelia Cotter, Chicago, Illinois*

spring rain again . . .
winds blow silver
in sunlight

~ *Charlotte Digregorio, Winnetka, Illinois*

sudden rain
singing in maple trees
red-breasted robins

~ *Frank J. Tassone, Montebello, New York*

afternoon tea
tulip bulbs outside
collect rain

~ *Kyle D. Craig, Indianapolis, Indiana*

equinox snow squall
pecking along the snowbank's edge
a robin

~ Deanna Tiefenthal, Rochester, New York

May downpour
husband walks home
shoes in his hand

~ Carolyn Noah Graetz, New Orleans, Louisiana

Spring's coffin cracked,
with the first raindrop falling
just out of nowhere

~ Zahra Akbar, Punjab, Pakistan

spring rain
the bomb hole fills up
with wildflowers

~ Victor P. Gendrano, Seal Beach, California

a blackbird drinks from the pothole first crocus

~ David Boyer, Stamford, Connecticut

dew drops
resting on a spider's web
spring morning

~ James D. Fuson, New Haven, Michigan

Buson's grave
a wet hydrangea
bows its head

~ *Kath Abela Wilson, Pasadena, California*

raindrop craters
dimple the dry soil
letter returned

~ *Ignatius Fay, Sudbury, Ontario, Canada*

on my umbrella
the pitter-patter
of summer morning

~ *Tomoko Hata, Winnetka, Illinois*

storm clouds
the cry of a shearwater
circles the sky

~ *Ernest J. Berry, Blenheim, New Zealand*

the sun
dying in the rain
campfire embers

~ *Margaret Rutley, Victoria, British Columbia, Canada*

summer drought
a crescent moon
holds the rain

~ *Lori Becherer, Millstadt, Illinois*

summer lightning
the dusty scent
of approaching rain

~ Carolyn M. Hinderliter, Phoenix, Arizona

flying rain
winkling its way up the valley
kingfisher's beak

~ Sheila K. Barksdale, Gainesville, Florida

One thunderclap
ushers in the driving rain —
Slicing bell peppers

~ Bob Oliveira, Bonita Springs Florida

champagne
for no good reason
sun shower

~ *Alanna C. Burke, Santa Fe, New Mexico*

long summer rains mixing the colors of hydrangea

~ *Beverly Acuff Momoi, Mountain View, California*

midsummer thunder —
raindrops dance across
parking lot puddles

~ *CaroleAnn Lovin, Clearwater, Florida*

soft rain
an earthworm
stretches its pink

~ Marilyn Appl Walker, Madison, Georgia

three fawns
return to the mist
summer solstice

~ Ann Magyar, Brighton, Massachusetts

Russian sage
stooped by the rain
so many regrets

~ Cyndi Lloyd, Riverton, Utah

parched . . .
in her kiss
sweet summer rain

~ William Scott Galasso, Laguna Woods, California

across wet grass pieces of dawn

~ Marian M. Poe, Plano, Texas

all day rain . . .
the slow drizzle of honey
from the dipper

~ Elinor Pihl Huggett, Lakeville, Indiana

after the rain
the folded umbrellas
of morning glories

~ *Mary Frederick Ahearn, Pottstown, Pennsylvania*

July morning
dewdrops on sunflowers
brown and gold

~ *Maureen Lanagan Haggerty, Madison, New Jersey*

first rain soothes
the dry rattle of leaves
my breath slows

~ *Eleanor Carolan, Felton, California*

beachpath
the sparkle of dew
on honeysuckle

~ *Patricia Harvey, East Longmeadow, Massachusetts*

summer rains . . .
the rising river
of daydreams

~ *Padma Thampatty, Wexford, Pennsylvania*

water droplets
rainbows
on a red tomato

~ *Genevieve Bergeson, Chesterfield, Missouri*

during the drought
Indian rain dance CDs
sold out

~ Henry W. Kreuter, Lebanon, New Jersey

barefoot on the blacktop puddle drum

~ Denise Fontaine-Pincince, Belchertown,
Massachusetts

This sundrenched morning
see how the rain has spoken
to the Ranger blooms

~ Philip Boatright, Tucson, Arizona

as if
the rain were not enough
a double rainbow

~ *Chandra Bales, Albuquerque, New Mexico*

summer heat
memorizing the sound
of rain

~ *Stevie Strang, Laguna Niguel, California*

on the horizon
another line of thunderheads
his volatile temper

~ *Mary Kipps, Sterling Virginia*

vacation home —
rain tapping on the skylight
in every room

~ *kjmunro, Whitehorse, Yukon Territory, Canada*

carefully negotiating
late summer's storm
sidestep puddles

~ *Malcolm Robert Willison, Schenectady, New York*

summer rain . . .
the squirrel grooms away
weeks of drought

~ *Gretchen Graft Batz, Elsah, Illinois*

summer rain
the pink lining of the crow's
open beak

~ *Connie Hutchison, Kirkland, Washington*

chestnut avenue
only the sound of rain
reaches the ground

~ *Anna Maris, Övraby, Tomelilla, Sweden*

night of heavy rain —
rising with the sun
fresh mushrooms

~ *Jill Lange, Cleveland Heights, Ohio*

wet leaves
the slippery path
of memory

~ *Gregory Longenecker, Pasadena, California*

without a sound
except the sliding door . . .
paws on wet leaves

~ *Thomas Sacramona, Plainville, Massachusetts*

autumn equinox
through the east window
sunshine in the shower

~ *Nan Dozier, Shreveport Louisiana*

October rain—
ten years tonight
since hearing your voice

~ *Antoinette Libro, Sea Isle City, New Jersey*

day's end . . .
the old well drawing down
autumn rain

~ *Gwenn Gurnack, Boston, Massachusetts*

the weight
of bobby pins
autumn rain

~ *Elmedin Kadric, Helsingborg, Sweden*

third day of rain
and hurricane winds —
one crow calls

~ Shirley A. Plummer, Yachats, Oregon

fog filled valley
the shape of a dog's bark

~ Joseph Robello, Novato, California

cold moon
ghostly mountain fog
surreal moonscape

~ Lyn Pizor, Pahrump, Nevada

autumn rain—
branches drop
their colors

~ Renee Londner, Prospect, Connecticut

second flood—
this time
I take my glasses

~ Susan Godwin, Madison, Wisconsin

haloed
by ice crystals
crescent moon

~ Art Elser, Denver, Colorado

light snowfall
on the tucked-in heads
of drifting seabirds

~ H.F. Noyes (1918 - 2010), Athens, Greece

under icicles dodging the jazz riffs of winter

~ Lori Zajkowski, New York, New York

incoming clouds
the snowman's
wide open arms

~ Michele L. Harvey Hamilton, New York

after the ice storm
branches heavy
with evening light

~ *Ben Moeller-Gaa, St. Louis, Missouri*

January thaw . . .
letting go
of old heartaches

~ *Ellen Grace Olinger, Oostburg, Wisconsin*

winter drought
the knees of a cypress tree
in sand

~ *Paula Moore, Jacksonville, Florida*

misty drizzle
the plover's footprints
becoming sand

~ *Lesley Anne Swanson, Coopersburg, Pennsylvania*

gliding
on the snow-covered lawn —
the hawk's shadow

~ *James Davis, Silver Spring, Maryland*

snow meadow —
knowing
not to tell her

~ *Mimi Ahern, San Jose, California*

the remaining snow
in isolated patches
our separate lives

~ *Patricia J. Machmiller, San Jose, California*

winter ice storm
riding the train home
—flowers on my lap

~ *Steven H. Greene, Haddon Township, New Jersey*

paw prints
on the snow cover
coyote moon

~ *Thomas Chockley, Plainfield, Illinois*

winter rain . . .
longing for warm grass
on my cheek

~ *Michael Sheffield, Santa Rosa, California*

battering ice storm
the garden buddha
loses face

~ *Marilyn Gabel, Agawam, Massachusetts*

noonday sun
glistens rippled blue shadows
sea of snow

~ *Von S. Bourland, Happy, Texas*

Old moon...new snow
 White Raven's shadow gliding
  into the new year

~ *Robert F. Mainone (1929 - 2015), Delton, Michigan*

white snow
a line drawing
on a barren hill

~ *Doris Ann Hayes; Burlington, Wisconsin*

winter rain
ends—umbrellas close
bulbs open

~ *Ellen Peckham, New York, New York*

late snow
the boots she left
under the bench

~ Sheila Sondik, Bellingham, Washington

sudden rain
no end to the universe
we know

~ Gary Hotham, Scaggsville, Maryland

steady rain
the dancer stretches
in long arcs

~ Miriam Borne, New York, New York

patter of rain . . .
I remember her
singing

~ Bonnie Stepenoff, Chesterfield, Missouri

every voice
reduced to small circles—
evening rain

~ Joshua Eric Williams, Carrollton, Georgia

rain all day
a place i cannot reach
in mother's eyes

~ Roberta Beary, Bethesda, Maryland

tree rain
learning to live with
a little less

~ *Michael Henry Lee, St. Augustine, Florida*

rain
    music
        in the trees
before I feel it

~ *Susan B. Auld, Arlington Heights, Illinois*

carrying
the sound of rain —
pink umbrella

~ *Pearl Pirie, Ottawa, Ontario, Canada*

those eyes
lost dog poster
dark with rain

~ Ann K. Schwader, Westminster, Colorado

only her eyes wet
the girl
in the black raincoat

~ Carlos Colon, Shreveport, Louisiana

driving his ashes home
the sweep
of the windshield wipers

~ Mark Forrester, Hyattsville, Maryland

steady rain
horses' hooves
ring on the asphalt

~ *Jennifer Sutherland, Glen Waverley, Victoria, Australia*

cool puddles
a stray laps up
the evening

~ *Roland Packer, Hamilton, Ontario, Canada*

the flow
of bodies through it —
city rain

~ *Bryan Rickert, Belleville, Illinois*

rain shadow
an old couple
hand in hand

~ *Dan Curtis, Victoria, British Columbia, Canada*

all our plans blown slanted rain

~ *Matthew Moffett, Mt. Pleasant, Michigan*

seventh day of rain . . .
trying to remember
the names of things

~ *Bill Pauly, Asbury, Iowa*

after the downpour
the evening sky
all over the road

~ *David Serjeant, Chesterfield, Derbyshire, United Kingdom*

rainy days . . .
a trip for more
bobbins

~ *D.W. Skrivseth, St. Anthony, Minnesota*

in your place
this rain bound for
west virginia
~ *John Martone, Charleston, Illinois*

baby's first rainstorm
the old scrap book
left on the porch

~ *Bryan Hansel, Grand Marais, Minnesota*

the condensed fog drops
-within the trees, rain forests-
spilling leaf to leaf

~ *Carolyn Bell, Trinidad, California*

majestic glacier
blue ice
melting

~ *Christine Wenk-Harrison, Lago Vista,
Texas*

Following the course
  of the raindrop intently—
    still it disappears.

~ Sydell Rosenberg (1929 - 1996), Queens, New York

A charter member of
the Haiku Society of America, 1968

Humanity

first day of spring . . .
his frozen footprints
still walking away

~ *Julie Warther, Dover, Ohio*

spring equinox
the time it takes
to not decide

~ *James Won, Temple City, California*

dancing with her
the smell of warm cotton
and fresh sweat

~ *David Oates, Athens, Georgia*

a quart per hour
in my hiking pack
the heft of thirst

~ *Autumn Noelle Hall, Green Mountain Falls, Colorado*

water lily
the way you close
your hands to pray

~ *Debbie Strange, Winnipeg, Manitoba, Canada*

summer stars
she bathes the baby
in a tin washtub

~ *Ferris Gilli, Marietta, Georgia*

congested sinuses
I fall asleep listening
to wet tire

~ Sidney Bending, Victoria, British Columbia, Canada

On paper
a startled haiku
still wet

~ Bruce England, Santa Clara, California

steam
unwrapping
her corn husk

~ Gabriel Patterson, Las Vegas, Nevada

drained
reflecting pool
a war forgotten

~ *Jon Hare, East Greenwich, Rhode Island*

smell of earth
water cannons now quell
an uprising

~ *Ajaya Mahala, Pune, Maharashtra, India*

baptismal candle
baby shuts her eyes
against the water

~ *Edward J. Rielly, Westbrook, Maine*

wishing well
an old woman
reaches in

~ *Jeremy Pendrey, Walnut Creek, California*

evacuating . . .
damp leaves cling
to the welcome mat

~ *Merle D. Hinchee, Houma, Louisiana*

icewater
the death announcement that
didn't startle me

~ *Oleg Kagan, Los Angeles, California*

reaching in his sport coat pocket
for a water balloon
family reunion

~ — *T56, Sewanee, Tennessee*

Prior Publications

Numbers in parentheses indicate anthology page numbers.

Banks, Caroline Giles (22), *Frogpond* 11.3, 1988.

Banwarth, Francine (64), *Acorn* 27, 2011.

Beary, Roberta (97), *Deflection*, Accents Publishing, 2015.

Berry, Ernest J. (75), 3rd place, Henderson Award, 1998.

Burns, Allan (38), *Acorn* 30, 2013.

Byrd, Peg McAulay (33), *Mariposa* 23, 2010.

Chauhan, Sandip (46), *In One Breath*, Unistar Books, 2013.

Colpitts, Sue (10), *Frogpond* 37.1, 2014.

Constable, Susan (8), *Acorn* 20, 2008.

Cook, Wanda D. (11), *Wisteria* 6, 2007.

Dancy, Carolyn Coit (54), *Contemporary Haibun On-line* 9.1, 2013.

Digregorio, Charlotte (71), Asahi Haikuist Network, March 15, 2013.

Deming, Kristen (18), *Frogpond* 36.1, 2013.

Dozier, Nan (86), *Frogpond* 23, 2000.

England, Bruce (108), *Blogging Along Tobacco Road*, May 30, 2012.

Feingold, Bruce H. (61), *Mariposa* 29, 2013.

Fleming, Marilyn (32), *Blithe Spirit*, May 2014.

Ford, Lorin (19), *Modern Haiku* 45.2, 2014.

Forges-Ryan, Sylvia (40), *Yale Anglers' Journal*, 10.2, 2009

Forrester, Mark (99), *Mayfly* 52, 2012.

Gendrano, Victor P. (73), *2nd Annual Basho Haiku Challenge Chapbook*, 2010.

Gilli, Ferris (107), *Modern Haiku* 43.2, 2012.

Gonzalez, John (61), *Presence* 46, 2012.

Gorman, LeRoy (36), *Kō*, 24.10, 2010.

Hart, William (39), *Monsoon: Poems Written in India and Nepal,* Timberline Press, 1991.

Haslett, Arch (31), *Time Haiku* 40, 2014.

Herrin, Poppy (28), 1st honorable mention, Tokutomi Memorial Contest, 2012.

Hotham, Gary (96), *Modern Haiku* 44.2, 2013.

Huggett, Elinor Pihl (79), *Haiku Canada*, 2014.

Jacobs, David (60), *Daily Haiku* Cycle 18, 2014.

Janjalija, Damir (53), *Simply Haiku* 10.2, 2012.

Kadric, Elmedin (87), *Modern Haiku* 45.3, 2014.

Kolodji, Deborah P (65), *Modern Haiku* 42.1, 2011.

Kozubek, S.M. (63), *Now This: Contemporary Poems of Beginnings, Renewals, and Firsts*, 2013.

Libro, Antoinette (87), *Wind Chimes*, November 1985.

Lloyd, Cyndi (78), *Sharpening the Green Pencil*, 2015.

Longenecker, Gregory (86), *A Hundred Gourds* 3.4, 2014.

Lukstein, Janis Albright (15), *Southern California Study Group Members Anthology*, 2014.

Machmiller, Patricia J. (93), *The San Francisco Haiku Anthology*, Smythe-Waithe Press, 1992.

Magyar, Ann (78), *Shamrock Haiku Journal* 29, 2014.

Makino, Annette (62), *Frogpond* 35.3, 2012.

Mason, Scott (42), *Modern Haiku* 44.2, 2013.

McKeon, Joe (48), *cattails*, May, 2014.

Moeller-Gaa, Ben (91), *A Hundred Gourds* 2.3, 2013.

Momoi, Beverly Acuff (77), *Daily Haiku* Cycle 17, 2014.

Muirhead, Marsh (8), *Modern Haiku* 39.3, 2010.

Newton, Peter (43), *The Heron's Nest*, 15.4, 2013.

Noyes, H.F. (90), *Between Two Waves*, Constanta, 1996.

Olsonn, Marian (54), *Hummingbird* 13.2, 2002.

Owen, Renée (39), *Mariposa* 24, 2011.

Packer, Roland (100), *Kokako* 21, 2014.

Painting, Tom (12), *Modern Haiku* 46.1, 20

Patchel, Christopher (41), *RawNervz* 9.1, 2003.

Pauley, Bill (101), *Frogpond*, 9.4, 1986; *Haiku Moment*, 1993.

Paulson, James A. (21), *bottlerockets* 3.2, 2002.

Penton, Ann M. (31), *TrailBlazer*, Summer 2001.

Poe, Marian M. (79), *Modern Haiku*, 44.1, 2013.

Robello, Joseph (88), *Frogpond* 31.3, 2008.

Robinson, Chad Lee (20), *Acorn* 23, 2009.

Rumpel, Lyle (56), *colours of thread*, CIES Media of the Canadian Institute For Enneagram Studies, 2012.

Schopfer, Olivier (47), *Chrysanthemum* 16, 2014.

Schwader, Ann K. (99), *Modern Haiku* 43.1 2012.

Seltzer, William (70), *Modern Haiku*, 44.3, 2013.

Serjeant, David (102), *Notes from the Gean* 3.2, 2011.

Snow, Barbara (32), Shiki Kukai, September 2013.

Sterba, Carmen (17), *The Heron's Nest* 5.4, 2003.

Strange, Debbie (107), World Haiku Association 122nd Haiga Contest, 2014.

Sutter, Dave (62), *Frogpond*, 1992.

Tate, Barbara (68), *Poet's Art* 53.14, date unknown.

Tennison, Michelle (36), *Modern Haiku*, 31.2, 2000.

van den Heuvel, Cor (9), *Suspiciously Small: A Collection of Haiku*, Spring Street Haiku Group, 2010.

Walker, Marilyn Appl (78), *The Heron's Nest* 10, 2004.

Watts, Lew (46), *Presence* 51, 2014.

Won, James (106), *Frogpond* 37.2, 2014.

Yarrow, Ruth (18), *Frogpond* 27.2, 2005.

Index of Poets

114

Made in the USA
San Bernardino, CA
03 November 2015